Contents

Introduction 5

In-line skating 9

Getting started 14

Who can become an in-line skater? 25

Who are the professional in-line skaters? . . . 33

In-line skating competitions 37

Quick facts about in-line skating 42

Glossary 44

Internet sites and addresses. 46

Books and magazines 47

Index 48

In-line skaters seek thrills by jumping off objects and doing tricks in the air.

In-line Skating

This book is due for return on or before the last date shown below.

www.raintreepublishers.co.uk

Visit our website to find out more information about **Raintree** books.

To order:
☎ Phone 44 (0) 1865 888112
📄 Send a fax to 44 (0) 1865 314091
💻 Visit the Raintree Bookshop at www.raintreepublishers.co.uk to browse our catalogue and order online.

First published in Great Britain by Raintree Publishers, Halley Court, Jordan Hill, Oxford, OX2 8EJ, part of Harcourt Education.
Raintree is a registered trademark of Harcourt Education Ltd.

Consultant: Kristine M. Simeone
Director, In-line Certification Program
International In-line Skating Association

Editor: Isabel Thomas
Cover Design: Michelle Lisseter
Production: Jonathan Smith

Originated by Dot Gradations Ltd
Printed and bound in China and Hong Kong by South China

ISBN 1 844 21288 2 (hardback)
07 06 05 04 03
10 9 8 7 6 5 4 3 2 1

ISBN 1 844 21293 9 (paperback)
08 07 06 05 04
10 9 8 7 6 5 4 3 2 1

British Library Cataloguing in Publication Data

A catalogue for this book is available from the British Library

Acknowledgements

The publishers would like to thank the following for permission to reproduce photographs:
Tony Donaldson: pp. **1, 8, 12, 17, 18, 21, 28, 30, 32, 39, 40, 42 top, 42 bottom, 43 top, 43 bottom**; Jack Gescheidt: pp. **4–5, 6, 14–15, 22, 24–25, 27, 34, 36**

Cover photograph reproduced with permission of Tony Donaldson.

Every effort has been made to contact copyright holders of any material reproduced in this book. Any omissions will be rectified in subsequent printings if notice is given to the publishers.

Introduction

Extreme sports are relatively new sports taken up by daring athletes. They are fun, but can also be dangerous. People who take part in extreme sports must do everything they can to be safe and avoid injury. In-line skating is an extreme sport that is growing more and more popular. In-line skaters ride on skates that have a row of wheels in a straight line underneath them. They might race, play roller hockey or use **ramps** and obstacles to do tricks.

You may have heard of the **X Games**, held every year in the USA. But do you know what a **half-pipe** is? Do you know how the roller skate led to the invention of the in-line skate? Who are the top in-line skaters in the world today? What do you need to do if you want to take up the sport? This book will answer all of these questions and more.

In-line skaters ride on pavements and paths in cities around the world.

How to use this book

This book is divided into parts called chapters. The title of each chapter tells you what it is about. A list of chapters and their page numbers appears in the table of contents on page 3. The index on page 48 gives you all the page numbers where you will find the main topics discussed in this book.

Each chapter has colourful photographs, captions and information boxes. The photographs show you some of the things written about in the book, so you will know what they look like. A caption is an explanation that tells you about a photograph. The captions in this book are in light blue boxes. Special boxes give you extra information about the subject.

You may not know what some of the words in this book mean. To learn new words, you should look them up in a dictionary. This book has a small dictionary called a glossary. Words that appear in **bold** type are explained in the glossary on page 44.

You can use the Internet sites listed on page 46 to learn more about the topics discussed in this book. You could e-mail some of the organizations listed, asking them questions or asking them to send you information.

This is pro in-line skater Matt Salerno at a competition doing tricks that are scored by judges.

In-line skating

In-line skating is a cross between ice skating and roller skating. Most in-line skates have four wheels in a single row. This allows in-line skaters to move over smooth surfaces like ice skaters move over ice. In-line skaters often ride on roads and pavements. They need to stay away from dangers, including cars, bicycles and other people.

Every week, in many major cities around the world, thousands of in-line skaters take to the streets for group skates. In some cities, so many skaters take part that marshalls and police are needed to direct them and stop the **traffic.** One of the biggest city skates in the UK takes place every Friday night around the streets of London.

Skating safely

The International In-line Skating Association (IISA) was founded in 1991 by skaters and skate makers. One of its aims is to teach people how to skate more safely. These are some of its suggestions for safe skating.

Skaters should be sensible and follow traffic laws.

Skaters should always wear helmets and knee, elbow and wrist pads, which must be in a good condition.

Skaters need to learn to stop and turn safely.

Skaters must follow the same traffic laws as cars and bikes.

Skaters should be polite to other skaters and also to people walking on the pavement. Skaters should pass other skaters only on the left. Before passing another skater, they should shout 'passing on your left'. Skaters should stop to let people walking on the street go past them.

Types of in-line skating

There are many types of in-line skating. Most people start skating for fun or to get fit. This is known as **recreational** skating. Some experienced in-line skaters enter races like runners do. Some racers skate on closed-off roads. Others, called speed skaters, skate around a special **track**.

Most ice-skating movements can also be done on in-line skates. This type of skating is called freestyle. Many in-line skaters also play roller hockey. This sport is like ice hockey on in-line skates. Roller hockey is played on a flat area of ground, such as an empty car park, with a hockey stick and a ball instead of a puck.

In-line skaters who do stunts are called aggressive skaters. They use ramps or rails to do tricks and jumps. **Street courses** are special places built for in-line skaters to practise. They have steps, street kerbs and railings for doing skating tricks.

These in-line skaters are playing roller hockey on their skates.

How in-line skating began

A Belgian man called John Joseph Merlin was the first person to make a pair of roller skates. In 1760, he attached wooden spools to his shoes. His skates did not work very well. He could not steer or stop and often crashed.

In 1863, an American man called James L. Plimpton made skates that worked better. He joined four wooden wheels to each of his shoes. He then put rubber over each wheel. The skates turned more easily, but it was still difficult to stop moving.

In 1960, the Chicago Skate Company built the first in-line skates. It was not easy to stay upright on them, and it was hard to stop because they did not have good brakes. In 1979, another American called Scott Olson saw a second-hand pair of these skates at a local shop. He thought he could use the skates in the summer to train for ice skating.

Olson attached better wheels and good brakes to the skates. This made them easier to steer and stop. In 1980, Olson and his brother Brennan started making their own skates. They formed the Rollerblade company. Other companies began making in-line skates too. More and more people began using them instead of roller skates. Skaters found that in-line skates allowed them to go faster and turn more easily.

Getting started

Helmets and pads protect skaters when they fall. They are as important as the skates themselves. All skaters should wear a **helmet** and pads whenever they skate.

A helmet is designed to protect a skater's head if he or she falls down. A helmet must fit well. Most helmets have a soft inside and a harder outer **shell**. Helmets should be approved by safety groups like the International In-line Skating Association (IISA).

Skaters should also wear elbow and knee pads to protect their skin and bones. These pads are soft on the inside with a hard shell on the outside. Like a helmet, pads need to fit well. If they do not, they can slip off during a fall.

Even very experienced in-line skaters wear helmets to protect their heads.

Wrist guards

Skaters injure their hands and wrists more than any other parts of their bodies. **Wrist guards** keep a skater's wrists straight during a fall. This reduces the chance of a hand or wrist injury. An injury is some kind of hurt or damage, like a broken bone or a sprain. A sprain means that one of the body's joints has been twisted, tearing the muscles or ligaments. A ligament holds together the bones in a joint.

Skates

Choosing the right skate is important for safety. Some in-line skates cost less than others do, but most of these inexpensive skates are not comfortable or easy to steer, which makes them less safe. Skaters could injure themselves by using these skates.

Skater profile: Cesar Mora

Cesar Mora is one of the best aggressive skaters in the world. He was born in Spain but grew up in Sydney, Australia. He won a gold medal in the X Games in 1998 and he won the Aggressive Skaters Association World In-line Championships later that year. Mora likes to teach other in-line skaters new tricks.

Professional in-line skater Takeshi Yasutoko takes a break at the X Games.

Some sports shops sell good quality second-hand skates for less money than new ones. These skates are usually safe and work well.

All in-line skates are made up of certain parts. The hard outside covering on a skate is called the shell. The shell covers the **boot**, which is the body of the skate.

This is pro in-line skater Chris Edwards using aggressive skates to do tricks.

Liners, frames and wheels

There is often a **liner** inside the boot. A liner is like a thick sock made of foam. A **frame** connects the wheels to the boot. Frames are made of plastic or metal.

In-line skate wheels are made of urethane, a type of plastic that can be made hard or soft. Skaters choose wheels based on the size and hardness best for their type of skating.

Choosing the right skate

Most in-line skaters buy **fitness skates**. These have a hard outer shell and four large wheels. They can be used for many different kinds of skating. Some skaters need to use special skates. Using the wrong skate for certain types of skating can be dangerous.

In-line skating timeline

1760: John Joseph Merlin puts wooden spools on his shoes to make the first roller skates

1863: James L. Plimpton invents a skate with rubber-covered wheels, which give a smoother ride

1960: Chicago Skate builds the first in-line skates

1980: Scott and Brennan Olson start the Rollerblade company to make in-line skates with good brakes

1995: The X Games begin

Other types of skate

Aggressive skates are designed to handle the stress of stunts and tricks. These skates have hard plastic or leather shells that cover the boot. They have thicker liners than fitness skates. They have four wheels, but these wheels are smaller than the ones on fitness skates. This makes the skates easier to steer.

Artistic skates are used for freestyle skating. The boots are quite like ice-skating boots. They have only three small wheels. The front and back wheels are softer than the middle wheel. This allows skaters to turn and spin smoothly.

Hockey skates are often made of leather and are tied with shoelaces. The shoelaces give a tighter fit. Hockey skates have four small wheels to make them easier to steer.

Speed skates have five large wheels to help skaters go faster. They have no brakes and are hard to turn.

Did you know?

The shape of your foot can help you decide which skates to buy. People with 'flat feet' will be more comfortable in hard fitness boots. If you have high arches, softer boots will be more comfortable. Skates should fit your feet closely, but leave enough room to wriggle your toes.

> ▲ This is pro skater Fabiola Da Silva doing
> a trick at the top of a half-pipe ramp.

Ramps and street courses

Aggressive in-line skaters do stunts using ramps and
street courses. Tricks done in the air are called
aerials. Skaters often grab hold of their skates while
they are up in the air. Most aerials are done using
ramps. A flip is a somersault done on the ground or
in the air. An invert is a handstand on a rail or the
side of a ramp.

> This is a typical in-line skating course at the X Games. Bundles of hay have been piled up to make a soft crash barrier.

Doing tricks

In-line skaters use three types of ramp for tricks. The most common is the **quarter-pipe**. It has one curved wall. Another ramp is the half-pipe, which has two curved walls and is shaped like a U. The third type of ramp is the **spine ramp**. It is made by placing two half-pipe ramps back to back.

Some in-line skaters practise their tricks on roads, pavements and in parks. Many people think this is dangerous for skaters, pedestrians and drivers. Some towns now have laws to stop skaters from doing tricks in public places.

Skaters also practise tricks on street courses. These are specially designed courses with steps, road kerbs and railings. Some also have ramps. Many towns now have these courses built just for people who do extreme sports like in-line skating, skateboarding and BMX biking.

Race tracks

In-line racing began in the 1980s. Most in-line racers skate around oval tracks. These racers are called speed skaters. Most speed skating tracks are between 100 and 200 metres long.

Some speed skaters also race on road courses. Public roads are blocked off during these races. The courses can cover very long distances.

Downhill in-line skaters race each other down steep hills. This is very dangerous. Downhill in-line skaters can earn a living from the prize money they win while racing.

In-line skaters should always wear clothing that will protect them if they fall.

Who can become an in-line skater?

Almost anyone can start skating if they are prepared. It helps to fairly healthy because skating is an energetic sport. Before beginning, new skaters need to buy the right skates and learn the safety rules. Then they can learn how to skate.

Stretching

Skaters use many muscles in their bodies, so it is important to stretch well before skating. Skaters who stretch do not get injured as often. They also feel more relaxed and awake while skating. You should stretch the muscles in your arms, legs and back before skating.

Skills to learn

New skaters need to practise a few simple moves. First you should find a flat piece of ground where you can learn how to stand on skates. Your feet should be shoulder-width apart, with the skates pointing straight out in front. The rest of your body should point straight ahead too. You must keep your head up at all times to see what is in front of you.

Skater profile: Matt Salerno

Matt Salerno was born in Sydney, Australia in 1978. He was World ASA champion in 1999 and won silver medals in the X Games in both 1998 and 1999.

This in-line skater at the X Games has used
a quarter-pipe ramp to flip upside down.

Beginner skaters go to competitions to watch professional skaters like Cesar Mora, above, doing tricks.

Starting and stopping

The first move is to push off with your left foot. You can then shift all your weight to your right foot and roll along on that foot. Next, bring your left foot next to, but just ahead of, your right foot. Now you can repeat the basic movement again, this time pushing off with your right foot and rolling along on your left foot.

New skaters have to learn how to stop using the heel brake. Most in-line skates have a heel brake on the right skate. You should move the brake to the left skate if that is more comfortable. To stop, push the skate with the heel brake forwards while moving. Then point the toe of that skate upwards until the brake touches the ground.

Turning and falling

The easiest way to turn is to move your legs wider apart and put your body weight on the skate opposite to the way you want to turn. This will make your skates turn in the direction you want.

New skaters also have to learn how to fall properly. By falling over in the right way and using protective pads, you can avoid serious injuries. If you lose your balance you should try and fall forwards, landing on your knees first and then your elbows. Your wrists should touch the ground last. Then make your body flat so you slide along the ground with your knees bent and your skates pointing up. Falling like this will make sure you scrape your pads instead of your skin.

This beginner has learned basic skills
and is trying them on a road where there
is no traffic.

Where can I train?

It is a good idea to get lessons from a qualified in-line skating instructor. Instructors can teach you the rules of skating. They can watch you and show you how to skate better. They can also teach you what to wear when skating and show you how to mend your skates.

The best way to find a skating instructor is through the International In-line Skating Association (IISA). You can find their website address in the list on page 46 of this book. The IISA has a list of qualified teachers around the world, including the UK and Australia. You will be able to find an instructor for any type of in-line skating, including aggressive skating, speed skating and roller hockey.

Skater profile: Sam Fogarty

Sam Fogarty was voted the best all round skater in the world by the Aggressive Skating Association in 1999 and 2000. He was born in Australia in 1980 and is known for performing very technical and difficult tricks.

Professional in-line skater Aaron Feinberg is doing a trick on a rail.

Who are the professional in-line skaters?

Fabiola Da Silva, known as 'Fabby', began skating in competitions in 1996. She is a **professional**, or 'pro'. This is a person who earns money for doing something that ordinary people do for fun. In her first three years, she won three gold medals in the **X Games**. These games were started in 1995 by a television network in the USA. Da Silva also won a gold medal at the 2000 X Games. Today, she is one of the most famous skaters in the world. She is often ranked by the ASA as the best female skater and now competes against men.

Aaron Feinberg is one of the best street-course skaters in the world. Feinberg won the men's in-line street finals at the X Games when he was only sixteen. Feinberg was born in the USA in 1981. He ranks high on the ASA Pro Tour and is one of the top five aggressive in-line skaters in the world.

These in-line skaters are racing
on a road course.

Practise

Like anyone else, Da Silva and Feinberg had to learn
how to skate. They began with the basics, practised
easy tricks and then more difficult ones. Today, Da
Silva and Feinberg make up their own tricks. These
new tricks help them win competitions. Each new
trick takes more practise and more hard work.

How to ride ramps

Skaters begin by skating across the ramp to build up speed. Then they skate up the wall of the ramp and jump into the air at the top. Skaters try to jump as high as they can. They call this **catching air**.

Street courses

Street skaters also use small ramps to do **aerials**. They do **grinds** by jumping up on to railings or road kerbs and dragging the wheels or frames of their skates across the railing or kerb. They often put **grind plates** on their skates to grind better. These metal or plastic plates fit onto the inside of skate frames.

Skater profile: Chris Edwards

Chris Edwards has been called the father of aggressive in-line skating. He invented many of the tricks used by aggressive skaters today. He began skating in competitions in the mid-1990s and has won many titles, including a gold medal in the X Games. In 1998, Edwards broke his arm and missed the entire skating season. The following year, he began skating in competitions again. He now competes less and instead teaches other people how to skate.

This skater at the X Games has used a ramp to catch big air and do a trick.

In-line skating competitions

The Aggressive Skaters Association (ASA) is the only international aggressive in-line skating group. It was founded in 1994 by a group of in-line skaters. Anyone can join.

The ASA runs the ASA Pro Tour. More than 150 skaters from over twenty countries compete for titles and money at differnt ASA competitions, including the ASA World Championships and the X Games.

Becoming a skater on the ASA Pro Tour is not easy. To do this, skaters must do very well on the ASA amateur tour first. Amateur skaters are people who skate for fun, not money. Amateurs must win national competitions in their home countries before they can move on to international competitions. The best skaters may make the ASA Pro Tour. More than 7000 amateur skaters compete for 30 open spots on the ASA Pro Tour each year.

Sponsors

Most skaters on the ASA Pro Tour make their living from skating. They skate in ASA competitions all year round. They are ranked on their performances. The top-ranked skaters compete in the X Games and World In-line Championships.

Competing in so many events involves a lot of travel and costs a lot of money. Most skaters could not do it without **sponsors**. A sponsor is a company that pays a skater to use or advertise its product. One well-known sponsor is Rollerblade, which sponsors Fabiola Da Silva. Rollerblade pays her to wear its skates.

Judging a trick

In street competitions, in-line skaters have a set amount of time to skate. Judges give them points for tricks. Harder tricks get more points. Judges also give points for style and for the number of obstacles skaters use.

In-line skaters also have a set amount of time to skate in ramp competitions. Judges give points for the number of tricks they do. Harder tricks get the most points. Judges also give extra points to skaters who catch the most air.

This in-line skater is racing down a slalom course on a dirt hill.

In-line skating is becoming popular for people of all ages.

Competitions and prizes

The X Games started in 1995. The USA television network ESPN has organized and shown these games every year since then. Many different extreme sports are performed at the X Games. The in-line skating competitions include men's and women's ramp events and men's and women's street events. Skaters from all over the world compete for gold, silver and bronze medals and also for prize money.

Skaters who make the ASA Pro Tour also compete for prize money. In 2002, Pro Tour events took place in Malaysia, Brazil, the USA and Spain.

In-line skating competitions are popular all over the world. Skaters are always making up new tricks. Skate makers are also making better skates. In-line skating remains one of the fastest growing extreme sports. It is the combined effort of people of all ages that makes it such a popular sport.

Quick facts about
In-line skating

- Dave Cooper and Eddie Matzger in-line skated up and down Mount Kilimanjaro, Africa's highest mountain, in 1998.

- About 50 per cent of in-line skaters are female.

- About 50 per cent of in-line skaters are over 18 years old.

- Some skiers practise by riding down steep hills on in-line skates.

- An in-line skater can burn 285 calories in 30 minutes and produce a heart rate of 148 beats per minute.

- Skating fast for one minute and then slowly for one minute can burn 450 calories if you skate for 30 minutes.

- Eito and Takeshi Yasutoko are brothers. In 2000, Eito won an X Games gold medal and Takeshi won a silver.

- More than 40,000 fans watched the 1998 ASA Pro and Amateur Championships in Las Vegas, USA.

- Skate wheels have a longer life if they are used regularly.

Glossary

aerial trick done while in the air

aggressive skate in-line skate designed for performing stunts and tricks

artistic skate in-line skate used for dancing

boot main body of an in-line skate

catching air when skaters jump as high as they can into the air off the top of a ramp

fitness skate in-line skate that can be used for many different kinds of skating

frame part of a skate that connects the wheels to the skate

grind to drag a skate across a road kerb or railing

grind plate metal or plastic plate attached to the frame of an aggressive in-line skate

half-pipe U-shaped ramp with two curved walls

helmet hard type of hat that protects a person's head if they fall

liner inside of an in-line skate boot

professional person who makes money doing something amateurs do for fun

quarter-pipe ramp with one curved wall

ramp curved surface used for freestyle tricks

recreational something done for leisure and fun

shell hard outer case of a helmet, skate boot or pad

spine ramp ramp made of two half-pipes placed back to back

sponsor company that pays someone to use what it sells or to advertise its product

street course group of ramps, kerbs, stairs and railings used for tricks

track course on which races take place

traffic cars, bicycles and people travelling on streets or pavements

wrist guard item worn to protect the hand and wrist

X Games popular extreme sports competition hosted by the USA sports television network ESPN

Internet sites

UK Inline Skate Instructor listing
www.inlineonline.co.uk/icp.htm

Skate UK
www.skateuk.net

UKskate.com
www.ukskate.com

Federation of Inline Speed Skating
www.inlinespeed.co.uk

Aggressive Skaters Association (ASA)
www.ASAskate.com

International In-line Skating Association (IISA)
www.iisa.org

Books and magazines

Extreme Sports: Inline Skating, Glidewell, Steve. Raintree, Oxford, 2003

Radical Sports: Inline Skating, Bizley, Kirk. Heinemann Library, Oxford, 1999

Unity Magazine
> This magazine includes news, features and photographs of aggressive skating events in Europe. You will also find reviews of in-line skating equipment and advice on improving your skills.

Index

aerial 21, 35

boot 17, 19, 20

frame 19, 35

grind 35
grind plate 35

half-pipe 5, 22
helmet 10, 14

ice skating 9, 13

liner 19, 20

professional 33, 41

quarter-pipe 22

ramp 5, 11, 21–23, 35, 38, 41
Rollerblade 13, 19, 38
roller hockey 11, 31
roller skating 9

shell 14, 17, 19, 20
speed skating 11, 21, 23
sponsor 38
street course 11, 21, 23, 35

track 11, 23

wrist guard 16

X Games 5, 16, 19, 26, 33, 35, 37, 38, 41, 43